"*Choosing Gentleness* holds the concentrated wisdom of decades of healing and helping others heal, distilled into profound heart-easing medicine."
— Sonia Connolly, author of *Wellspring of Compassion* and *Presence After Trauma*

"Robyn helps us see how culture and family trauma create beliefs and behaviors that harm us and make us feel bad/wrong when we are different from the 'shoulds' we've been taught. Shining light on these harmful 'norms' lets us choose to love ourselves exactly as we are, no matter what others may think."
— Julie Levin, MFT, Marriage & Family Therapist, Pleasant Hill, CA

"The book's focus on radical self-acceptance reminds us of the importance of letting in and acknowledging our own shadow-side."
— Myrna Fleishman Ph.D., Psychotherapist/artist, Santa Barbara, CA

"Our society is a supersaturated solution of experts, books and YouTube videos claiming to help you feel better about yourself and navigate your way through the labyrinth of thoughts, feelings and sensations that make up anyone's life. What distinguishes Robyn's beautiful new book, *Choosing Gentleness*, from the rest of the pack is her ability to weave self-compassion into lives that have been inundated with unhelpful societal tropes."
— Nicole S. Urdang, M.S., NCC, DHM, LMHC, Holistic Psychotherapist, Buffalo, NY

"*Choosing Gentleness* offers thoughts and graphics that encourage you to find routes (roots) within yourself that are loving, kind, supportive, and above all, authentic to you."
— Vivian Sudhalter, Professional Editor/Wordsmith

"This is a delicious book full of bite size nuggets of wisdom on how to be kind to yourself."
— Caitlin E. Matthews, D.C., Chiropractor, Ojai, CA

What reviewers have written about Robyn's first book,
*Go Only as Fast as Your Slowest Part Feels Safe to Go: Tales to
Kindle Gentleness and Compassion for Our Exhausted Selves*

"The material and stories in this book are beautiful and riveting, rich in wisdom and compassion, at once healing and exciting. I think this book will fill you with the hope of having the life you were born to live and the life you've dreamed of, because this book is about our souls and hearts; about peace, gladness, and freedom."

— Anne Lamott, *New York Times* bestselling author of *Stitches,
Traveling Mercies, Bird by Bird,* and many others

"Robyn's work and words are deeply beneficial and instructive to all who feel less than self-loving or caring. You will find shelter and wings in the tender ferocity of these words that offer a sturdy platform of support and wisdom for people who wish to experience true self-love and care."

— SARK, author and artist of *Succulent Wild Woman,
Eat Mangoes Naked, Transformation Soup,
Glad No Matter What,* and many others

"If your inner critic has been working overtime, if other people's opinions are more important to you than your own, if you would like to learn how to soothe yourself in times of stress and distress, pick up this book."

— Nicole S. Urdang, M.S., NCC, DHM, LMHC,
Holistic Psychotherapist, Buffalo, NY

What reviewers have written about Robyn's journaling workbook,
Tenderly Embracing All the Ways that I Feel and Am: Journaling to Kindle Gentleness and Compassion for Our Precious Selves

"This journal workbook could be one of the most important books you'll ever hold, because it will also hold you. Robyn Posin's words, unobtrusive thoughts and beautiful life-giving wisdom will be like a midwife for you, if you are anything like me, helping you gently bring forth your own truth, and being, and self. Take my advice—and a long deep breath—and begin the journey of a lifetime."

— Anne Lamott, *New York Times* bestselling author of *Stitches,*
Traveling Mercies, Bird by Bird, and many others

"Robyn's wise and thoughtful words on the pages of this journal invite you to write your way to a deeper acceptance of yourself. Each page will take you to your core. Exploring the possibilities that Robyn offers here will help you to hear and embrace all of your self. This book could become your best friend."

— Myrna Fleishman, Ph.D., Psychotherapist/artist. Santa Barbara, CA

"This journal is like your best friend inside, came out and made a book for you! Robyn's tender and soul nourishing wisdom weaves throughout and you will feel guided and supported to explore and discover all that you are and what you feel. Going inward with this book will lead you to develop even more exquisite self-care, self-acceptance and self-LOVE."

— SARK, author and artist of *Succulent Wild Woman,*
Eat Mangoes Naked, Transformation Soup,
Glad No Matter What, and many others

Other books by Robyn L. Posin:

Go Only as Fast as Your Slowest Part Feels Safe to Go:
Tales to Kindle Gentleness and Compassion
for Our Exhausted Selves

Tenderly Embracing All the Ways that I Feel and Am:
Journaling to Kindle Gentleness and Compassion
for Our Precious Selves

Choosing Gentleness

Opening Our Hearts to All the Ways
We Feel and Are in Every Moment

Robyn L. Posin, Ph.D.

Compassionate Ink
Box 725
Ojai, CA 93024

Compassionate Ink
Box 725
Ojai, CA 93024

Copyright © 2018 by Robyn L. Posin, Ph.D./Compassionate Ink

All rights reserved. Published in the United States of America. No part of this book may be used or reproduced in any manner whatsoever without written permission from the publisher except in the case of brief quotations embodied in critical articles or reviews. For information contact Robyn L. Posin, Compassionate Ink, Box 725, Ojai, CA 93024

Cover Design by Catherine Baker with Barbara Fosbrink
Cover Photo by Barbara Fosbrink
Book Design by Catherine Baker with Barbara Fosbrink and Robyn L. Posin
Author Photo by Barbara Fosbrink

Publisher's Cataloging-in-Publication data
Names: Posin, Robyn L. author.
Title: Choosing gentleness: opening our hearts to all the ways we feel and are in every moment / Robyn L. Posin, Ph.D.
Description: Ojai, CA: Compassionate Ink, 2018.
Identifiers: ISBN 978-0-9891394-4-1 | LCCN 2018906241
Subjects: LCSH Self-esteem. | Self-acceptance. | Compassion--Psychological aspects. | Self-actualization (Psychology) | Awareness. | Emotions. | Self-perception. | BISAC SELF-HELP / Emotions | BODY, MIND & SPIRIT / Inspiration & Personal Growth | Classification: LCC BF511.P66 2018 | DDC 152.4--dc23

PRINTED IN THE UNITED STATES OF AMERICA

With so much love and gratitude to the Grandmothers:
the multi-racial, multi-ethnic, zany and outrageous
band of ancient spirit beings that continue to guide,
nudge and protect me as they whisper in my heart
and gift me with words and images
along the way of my journey.

"You are never too sensitive, too serious, too particular, too fill-in-the-blank. What you may be is: more sensitive, more serious, more particular, more fill-in-the-blank than the people you're around feel comfortable with. Consider not being with them at such times!"

"The thing to do with feelings is to make it safe to feel all of them!"

From *The Rememberings and Celebrations Cards:*
Loving Reminders of the Great Mother's Voice

— Robyn L. Posin

Contents

Acknowledgments

I'm forever grateful to the Grandmothers, the zany collection of ancient female spirits that have been my mentors, protectors and supporters since I first met them in an awake dream in 1984. The images and accompanying poems in the pages ahead have come as gifts from these dear beings over the years since that first (conscious) encounter. They've tasked me to midwife their messages of compassionate wisdom into forms that could be shared in a world that sorely needs reminding of this gentle path.

Barbara Fosbrink—treasured friend, sister-on-the-path, patient mentor to me in creative collaboration, technologic competence, book design and what she calls "the view from 20,000 feet"—has, through almost 30 years of our separate and interwoven journeying, been committed to helping move the Grandmothers' messages out into the world. The gratitude I feel to this extraordinarily multi-talented woman exceeds any words I could find to describe it. This book and the two that preceded it (*Go Only as Fast as Your Slowest Part Feels Safe to Go* and *Tenderly Embracing All the Ways that I Feel and Am*) would never have emerged without her support, involvement and willingness to put up with my not-infrequent crankiness about incorporating her usually invaluable input. Our relationship has opened me to the possibilities and joys of creative collaboration—something I'd never before considered.

Since those books were published, Barbara (as always, with the Grandmothers' support) continued to nudge me into writing several short essays for the Compassionate Ink Facebook page that she's been intermittently managing. Those essays also live in the pages ahead. The photo of my resting place that graces the front cover and the photo of me on the back cover are both from her eye and camera. Once again, this is a book that would never have been born without her caring and committed midwifery.

When it became clear that we needed a graphic designer who could digitize my collection of pen and ink images as well as prepare the manuscript for CreateSpace publication, Barbara invited her friend, Catherine Baker—graphic designer extraordinaire—into our creative circle. Catherine's awesome skills, quirky sense of humor and delightful personality add much to our collaboration circle. Our combined energies are deliciously magical: a source of much ongoing amazement and amusement for all of us.

Once again, my dear friend Vivian Sudhalter, professional wordsmith and self-described OCD (obsessive compulsive) pedant, brought her hilarious New York sense of humor and eagle-eyed line editing to the manuscript.

We've moved only as fast as our slowest parts have felt safe (or free) to go as we've walked this book into its current form. Agreeing that setting deadlines would only (as inevitably it does) guarantee stress and tension, we chose to trust the birth to happen in its own organic time and it has. Being open to the book's own timing has allowed our various illnesses, traumatic injuries and periods of stagnation along the way to just be what was so in the moment rather than frustrating interruptions to some arbitrarily preset schedule. It's been great fun!

Introduction

In each of us, often deeply buried and inaccessible, lives a vibrant, inviolable creature self, the pure essence of who we truly are. When not interfered with, this Deep Self—our wise and knowing simple animal being—unerringly, instinctively moves us toward that which grows and nurtures us. Just as unfailingly, it moves us away from all that endangers us on any level.

The whole process of socialization in our so-called modern western culture, and much of what currently pass as paths to spiritual enlightenment, are essentially curricula that alienate us from our inner knowing and our authentic feeling-selves. They set external standards for what behaviors and emotions are acceptable/appropriate, embedding us in values and prescriptions that undermine, deny or contradict the credibility of these inner urgings. We learn that valuing ourselves requires adhering to these templates.

When we feel things or are moved to act in ways that we've learned we shouldn't, we give ourselves a bad time. We may judge, criticize or shame ourselves. Alternatively, we may try to deny how we feel. Despite all of these attempts to suppress what naturally rises up in us, whatever it is continues to press for recognition, acceptance. We feel disoriented and out-of-sorts as the life force of our essential self pushes to break through these externally imposed strictures.

It takes strong intention and conscious commitment to undo the noxious training, to honor what that life force asks of us. The path we take: questioning what we've been encouraged by our feelings-phobic culture to believe as truth; resisting the pressure to always do more, bigger, faster and be-done-yesterday in order to be valued; choosing, instead, to listen to our inner knowings and to make it safe and acceptable to feel all of our feelings.

To support this journey, the Grandmothers have gifted me annually with a drawing and words (now cards) that are powerful, empowering reminders of truths that are more healing. Always, these messages encourage—despite all we've been taught—permission to make it safe for, to keep opening our hearts to and compassionately embracing all the ways we might feel and/or be in every moment, even when we are being our less-than-most-shining selves.

In the pages ahead, you'll find these cards reproduced and interwoven among a group of essays that have emerged in the past five years since my two earlier books, *Go Only as Fast as Your Slowest Parts Feels Safe to Go: Tales to Kindle Gentleness and Compassion for Our Exhausted Selves,* and its companion journal/ workbook, *Tenderly Embracing All the Ways That I Feel and Am: Journaling to Kindle Gentleness and Compassion For Our Precious Selves,* were published.

My wish is that this collection will inspire and support you in the practice of being more gentle, compassionate and tender with your precious self—as much of the time as you possibly can.

Ojai, California
Summer 2018

P.S. At the back of the book, the Appendix provides information about my earlier books and other resources I produce to support this practice and the journey.

Something to consider about arrogance

An incredibly important life lesson I learned—though *not* from the course-work—while I was watching the goings on and posturing among both faculty and students in my graduate school Ph.D. program:

The degree of someone's arrogance is directly proportional to their degree of insecurity.

Keeping this in mind when dealing with arrogant people can defuse a great deal of the irritation and outrage such behavior often stirs in us.

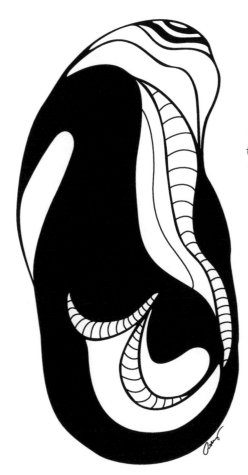

In the very center of the heart
of the long abandoned Child Within
lies the seed source, the birthing place
of the Ancient One, the mighty,
the protective Wise Woman
within us all.

So it is only by reclaiming and lovingly tending
the vulnerability of that undernourished Child
that we come to awaken and reveal
our greatest power.
And, in the strength of
that interdependence acknowledged
lies the incredible strength in vulnerability.

Reaching toward the heart of the Child,
we open to the return of the Great Mother:
the primordial, powerful female energy
we so need to heal ourselves
and our planet!

Reach, now!

3

Tenderly, with so much love,
I practice embracing my self
in the difficult, trying,
edge-walking times of crisis…

When I'm feeling anxious, lost, afraid, isolated or overwhelmed, I remember to remind my self that I am never alone on this journey: the Grandmothers are always with me, no matter how it may seem in the moment.

When I'm feeling paralyzed with the fear of making a mistake, I remember to remind my self that every choice I make is the best one I can make with the knowing I have at this moment. I remind my self that no choice I make is ever a mistake, even when I later come to see my options differently. I remember that what I choose now is for now, I can reconsider and re-choose whenever, as soon as, and as often as I need.

When something doesn't seem to be happening how or when I think it ought to, I remember to remind my self that it's likely that the Grandmothers have a vision and a timing for the process that's larger than my own limited view. I remind my self, in such times of frustration, both to have my rant and to practice surrendering (with trust) into the larger field.

When I'm feeling pushed or pressed, I remember to remind my self that no matter how it may seem, there is *no rush!* I remind my self that I can always allow my self to move only as fast as the slowest part of me feels safe to go. And, I remind my self that this is the only pace that's safe for me.

No matter what anyone else advises and despite whatever knowledge and authority they have or I have given them, I remember never to do anything that doesn't feel absolutely right in my belly. I remind my self that I am always and forever the world's greatest authority on me – when I listen to my belly.

When the story being told (by me or anyone else) makes me feel that I am bad, wrong, inadequate, shameful, or less than acceptable just as I am right now, I remember to remind my self that it can only be a lie. I remind my self to look always for the story that allows me to feel that it's absolutely okay to be as I am right now, even as I am still a work-in-progress continuing to grow, change and evolve.

When what I'm doing (listening to) makes me feel anxious or stressed, I remember to remind my self that either it's the wrong thing to be doing (listening to) or, it's the wrong time to be doing (listening to) it. I remind my self that I always have my own permission to stop doing (listening to) whatever it is. So, I do stop: *right now!*

When looking ahead makes me feel anxious, overwhelmed or frantic, I remember gently to bring my self back to just this smallest slice-of-now. I remind my self that the who I am becoming as I journey through this now will always be better prepared to cope with what may come later.

Please stop trying to make me feel better!

So often, in our emotion-phobic culture, when we choose to share about how upset, distressed, frustrated or angry we may be feeling in the moment, the people who love and care about us immediately respond with attempts to help us feel better. They lovingly offer reframes of the disturbing circumstances, remind us of how we've managed to come through such circumstances in our past, repeat platitudes (everything that doesn't kill us makes us stronger/everything happens for a reason) and/or they move directly into attempts to problem-solve for us ("what if you...," "have you tried...."). Never mind that all we might truly be needing/wanting in the moment is to have our intense feelings compassionately witnessed as we vent them.

Though my own small circle of intimate friends know better than to do any of these things when I share such feelings, my clients regularly report experiencing these responses to the sharing of their upsets. While such responses may frustrate or irritate them, they find it hard to tell the folks responding this way that they should stop. After all, "they mean well," or "they're only trying to help me" or "they're saying these things out of love for me."

I see it differently. When we share intense emotion, its energy is like a tuning fork: it resonates similar emotion in the person listening to us. If they aren't in touch with or are actively avoiding that emotion in themselves, listening to us stirs up unpleasant/disturbing waves in their psyches. Their attempts to "help *us* feel better" may, more likely, be seen as their attempts to shut down the feelings in us that are resonating so unpleasantly in them so that *they* can feel better! If we stop feeling/sharing what we're feeling, they'll feel better—things inside them will settle back down. Rather than caring selflessness, their words are more likely (if less than consciously) meant to take better care of their own stirred up selves. Even as I understand this often knee-jerk behavior and can feel compassion for the pain in these listeners that moves them to respond as they do, I hate it!

When, years back, I experienced this kind of shutting-down/supposed-caring, I'd feel like I wanted to scream. In the guise of being caring, these listeners were essentially asking me to take care of them/their sensitivities rather than stay with my own upset. Now, I know to say something like "if it's uncomfortable for you to be around my upset, it's really okay for you not to stay and listen. I need just to be with what I'm feeling right now and complain/vent. I need not to 'feel better' until I'm good and done with feeling my upset."

I think here of the advice I've offered to young therapists I've mentored over the years:

> The biggest gift you can give to a client is to listen to them with compassion and curiosity about how they're feeling—not to get into fixing them.

> Everyone moves/grows (and has a right to do so) at his/her very own pace. It is not their job to move at a pace that makes you feel effective.

> Growth and healing takes time and it's an inside job that you can only support, not make happen.

> And, if you don't feel comfortable working with someone, let them know you don't have the experience/expertise to be of help to them and then support them in the process of getting to someone else who does.

It seems to me this is equally good advice to anyone wanting to be a caring friend to someone who's dealing with challenging feelings/circumstances. When your friend's situation leaves you feeling helpless, remember that simply listening with compassion is an enormous gift. Often a "this really sucks!" or a "poor honey!" is incredibly comforting. And, (if you're so inclined), imagining them surrounded with love and light and the good energies of their spirit-helpers/guardians/angels as they navigate the turbulence can be a helpful thing to do with your concern. Always best to offer to help problem solve only if they ask for your input.

Coping with feeling overwhelmed

The other morning, coming in from my tent (where I sleep year round except in rain or windy weather), I noticed how much deadheading needed to be done in my container garden and how much leaf litter the wind the day before had blown all over the patio around the pots. The nine hummingbirds feeders hanging on the cottage eaves, all empty or almost empty, clearly needed washing and refilling.

Once in the cottage door, it was obvious my kitties had had a rambunctious night: tufts of cat hair were everywhere the eye could see. A vase on one of my altars had been knocked over. Though it hadn't broken, there was water, along with rose petals and fern droppings, on the bookcase and floor.

Since I'd slept in later than usual, the kitties were all over me complaining loudly, winding around my feet and almost tripping me as I headed to the counter to get their bowls. I had a fit! (They no longer scatter to hiding when I start raging: over our many years together, they've gotten used to my periodic and loud meltdowns.)

I stomped around, "f_ _k, f _ _king!" (Curse words are sooo relieving when I feel crazed and overwhelmed.) Yelling: "I hate this!" and "This is too much!" and "I need a clone!" and "I can't stand this!" and "I want a mommy!" Furious and in tears at the very same time, I felt completely beside my self. As always, the ranting and crying are intense for a time and then, like a switch getting thrown, the eruption is over.

Nothing's changed, all of the everything-needing-to-be-done is still there, but I'm in a different place. I begin to tackle the tasks one by one. Not thinking another thought about all there is to do, not reciting/rehashing the list in my head. I simply start moving and doing: staying in the thinnest slice of now, focusing only on whatever chore I'm addressing in just that moment, breathing deeply and feeling calm.

Along the way of my journey toward taking really good and loving care of my self, I've learned that it's not only okay but incredibly helpful to rant and rave (by my self, in safe space) when I feel put upon or overwhelmed. It never goes on for very long; I'm sure that's because I have my own full permission (without any judgment) to go for it when it surges up in me. I no longer even think of berating my beleaguered self with "Why are you wasting energy, you know you're just going have to do all it anyway!" Or, with "What's the point, it's not going to change anything!" The truth is, making room to feel the feelings actually changes everything.

What experience has taught me is that these ranting, tearful meltdowns release the energy of the overwhelm. Once the energy is released, we can come to calmness and surrender into whatever it is we have to deal with. When we don't allow for the releasing, we have to spend other energy suppressing the rage, energy we could better use, post-meltdown, for coping with what needs doing.

Our world, life swirling
turbulent, out of control
at the edge of the abyss.
Emotional white water
overwhelm:
feeling helpless,
powerless, anguished,
awash in fearful frustration,
despair.

No resistance possible.
Breathing deeply,
yielding to the vortex,
howling in rage, terror, grief.

Surrender takes us deeper:
through the center
to our center.
In exhausted stillness
knowing is reborn,
direction revealed.

In the turbulent times,
try living
in the thinnest slice of now
that you can define.
And, remember
to practice being
extravagantly gentle
with your very
precious self.

17

We cannot outrun them,
times of darkness always come.
Whoever teaches us that it's possible
to live always in the light, lies:
where there is light, shadows fall,
where there is day, night follows.

Uncertainty, upheaval, confusion, turmoil,
decline, death, loss, fear,
longing, pain:
these are not signs of failure.
They are signs of life unfolding.

What we run from,
grows its power over us.
What we risk to welcome,
what we risk to embrace,
what we risk to explore,
empowers us and brings us knowing.

There is no escaping darkness.
There is only the practice
of learning to hold ourselves
more safely
in the middle of its cycles.

Staying with darkness
when it comes,
our eye adjusts.
We can discover
radiance
within the dark.
We can grow new
ways of seeing.
We can find
new, more solid
ground.

As wind is given voice by the shape of each tree
through which it blows,
so Spirit is given voice by the shape of each of us
through whom it flows.

Gently pruning away the dense tangle
of inner branches,
the arborist opens a tree's heart
to the nourishing flow of wind, unobstructed.

Gently pruning away the dense tangle
of constraint, should and expectation,
we open our own heart
to the nourishing flow of Spirit, unobstructed.

The endless lesson repeats:
letting go, letting flow.

Hearing our inner voices

1: The impact of outside voices

We are all, to some greater or lesser degree, affected by living in a crazy-making, too-busy, out-of-balance world where the cultural trance of more, bigger, faster, do-it-yesterday sets the bar for what makes us feel worthy. Media images of success and beauty bombard us daily, liminally and subliminally, with idealized and photoshopped standards against which we are encouraged to measure our selves. Inevitably, our merely human selves fall short of these impossible standards. It's a world that is feelings-phobic, particularly averse to any emotions of the so-called dark or shadow sort (namely, anything other than joy or bliss.) Is it any wonder that even those of us fortunate enough to have had fairly positive parenting in our families of origin frequently find our selves dealing with the sense that we're either not enough or too much to be considered worthwhile or lovable.

We may hide our sadness or depression in order not to be seen as a "downer," a pariah. We may feel ashamed or guilty about the slightest bit of anger or rage— it's so not what nice girls should feel or else it's so "unevolved." And, particularly poisonously, some currently popular New Age flap would have us believe that letting our selves feel any so-called negative emotions will only attract more of the same. Therefore, this framing insists, we should avoid such at all costs. Never mind that stuffing them can wreak havoc in our bodies and psyches!

2: The impact of our family of origin

In addition to these external societal and cultural pressures, many of us were raised in dysfunctional families by damaged caregivers. These caregivers had little or no patience, room or permission for us to be allowed to cry ("You better stop that crying before I give you something to cry about!") or to be cranky, have a tantrum or an angry outburst ("You go to your room, young lady, until you can act civilly!").

We have rarely gotten to experience the truth about feelings. Namely, that they are the energy of life, neither good nor bad in themselves, meant to be felt and expressed (safely). That all feelings, when allowed, have a natural trajectory: they build to a crescendo and then diminish and fall away.

Those of us raised by damaged caregivers—who often had little tolerance for the normal neediness of their children—learned very early to do without support and to believe that any needfulness was shameful. To be safe, we cut off from, suppressed or abandoned these needy, upset, sad or angry parts of our selves; unattended, they live on hidden away inside of us.

3: The challenges of these influences

The pressures and prohibitions from the larger culture and from our family of origin get internalized, becoming a less than conscious template for acceptable behavior; an internalization of myriad external voices becomes a chorus drowning out our own authentic inner realities. We lose any sense of our center. When we step out of line, these internalized voices harangue us to make sure we shape up so that we'll be safe from external retribution. These critical voices, meaning to protect us, are themselves often painfully harsh and punitive.

Freeing our selves from the tyranny of these now-internalized oppressive voices is a process that begins with observing their messages rather than taking them in, believing them and being directed by them. It helps to explore and try to identify the source/lineage of any inner voice that makes us feel diminished or not-okay. Giving each such voice a name (e.g., the Hatchet Lady, the Judge, the Slave-Driver, the Production Manager) allows us to see our selves as separate from it. With journaling, we can enter into dialog with each voice and uncover what purpose it believes it serves, what it fears and from what it is trying to protect us.

In this dialog, we are liberating and connecting more fully with the voice of our own wise, inner-knowing self. From this self, we can begin to address those fears, transform those undermining influences and build loving, gentle support for the truths of our own inner knowing. And, we can begin to find ways to open our hearts to the needy, upset, sad or angry parts of our selves that, till now unat-tended, live on hidden away inside of us.

Growth unfolds as a spiraling journey

Surrounded, as we are, by our more, bigger, faster, done-yesterday culture, we've been misled into believing that growth is a linear process. With that mindset as backdrop, whenever we find we're confronting issues we thought we'd resolved some time ago, we give our selves a bad time. We criticize our selves for being naïve/dumb enough to have thought that we actually were done with whatever it was. Or, feeling deeply disappointed, we're likely to berate our selves for being back in the same old mess, yet again. Either way, we treat our vulnerable selves with unforgiving harshness at a time when we're already in distress and in need of gentleness and compassion.

The truth about growth, however, is that it is a spiraling journey. We come into this life with certain fixed points, the issues we are here to work with/on this time around. Our journey takes us on a spiral path that rises within a perimeter (as it were) defined by these fixed points. It helps to visualize the path we're on as a vertical coiling spiral rising between bamboo poles that rise from the earth up to the sky at several points around the compass.

As we resolve the versions of our issues that confront us at a particular level of the spiral, we get to cruise there for a while—just until we're ready to cross the threshold into the next turn of the spiral. There, the newest version of who we have become gets to pass through the circuit of a yet newer iteration of our fixed issues. In this threshold cycle, we learn whatever we need to in order to resolve this iteration of our issues with the current level of our consciousness. Once we do that work, we get to cruise for a while at this new level before the whole threshold process begins again.

As we continue traveling on the spiral path of growing (one can see it as moving upward or moving deeper) the iterations of our essential-this-lifetime issues get more and more attenuated and we move through to resolving these versions more and more rapidly and easily at each turning.

Holding this spiraling view of growth, the reappearance of some new version of our re-cycling fixed issues becomes a signal that we're at a threshold, about to move into a new level of consciousness—something to celebrate even as we do our work. How different this view is from one that would have us believing their appearance to be a sign that we've slipped-into-old-stuff-again. We practice treating our precious selves gently and with great compassion in these threshold times.

Some further reflections on how we grow

In a Developmental Psychology class way back in the early days of graduate school, I remember learning about the Gestalt Theory of the stages of child development. The notion (at least as I remember it) was that as a child kept on assimilating new information/skills, its existing organization would keep expanding/shifting to accommodate to these newly added bits. Then, at some critical moment, the being's organization would no longer be able to accommodate the just-one-more-new-bit. At that point, the existing organization would come undone. The child's behavior would seem to regress for a while.

This coming apart of the existing order would allow for a whole new organization to assemble itself and for the child to suddenly take a giant step forward to a new level of skill and competence. The form of this emergent order would not only incorporate the new bit but would be capable, for a while, of continuing to assimilate other new bits until another critical moment arrived and it would have to disassemble and form yet a newer organization. [Somewhere in my old journals,

I remember writing a poem (Coming Apart to Come Together) that was about this very process as it continues on into our adult lives. I know it well.]

For many years I would be perplexed by the arrival, seemingly out of the blue, of the periods of considerable discomfort that still arrive these days (though they no longer perplex me). At these times, I feel exhausted for no obvious external causes. I feel out of sorts, irritable, uncomfortable in my own skin. I go through not being able to find a place for my self. I wander around much like a dog circles and circles around as it tries to find the right spot to curl up in. I feel whiny, antsy, lost, teary for no apparent reason (much like I used to feel when premenstrual). Often, these are times when I find my self unexpectedly doubting or questioning the choices I've made in my life, choices about which I'm usually quite clear as having been right for me. These old life issues resolved at earlier times reappear in new guises; the Hatchet Lady's critical voice, long ago defanged, reappears grumbling some versions of very old litanies.

I can't remember when I first understood what these periods were about but, when they arrive these days (as they do still, from time to time), I recognize them for what they are: threshold times. Times when my old way of being is coming undone to make way for some new organization of me to emerge. The pieces come apart so that they can reassemble in a new way for the next season of my unfolding. These interludes are still uncomfortable but, once I recognize them for what they are, they're no longer so disquieting. Most times it takes a few days before I'm onto what's going on and, occasionally, these between-times do last a while. I've learned to be exceedingly tender and loving with my prickly self during such threshold/transition times, to not ask very much from me and to do a lot of resting. The next step/new way always emerges at just the right moment. I've learned to trust that and not push my self. It's how we all can better deal with the threshold times in the spiraling journey of growing.

May you be blessed with:

An ever-increasing awareness
of who and how you truly are,

An ever-expanding capability
to compassionately embrace
all of who you are,

An ever-blossoming ability
to live from your deepest truths,

An ever-burgeoning capacity
to give and receive love,

An ever-growing facility
for experiencing delight
and contentment.

Welcoming our sorrow, anger, fear,
despair, jealousy and hate
as open-heartedly
as we do our joy, delight,
excitement, elation and love —
allows these intense feelings
room to swell, crest,
reveal their teachings
and naturally fade away.
This always moves us forward.

When others' or our own critical voices
label such emotions negative or bad-for-us,
the self-nurturer inside of us practices
embracing our challenging feelings
with ever greater tenderness
and compassion.

We honor the deepest truth:
it is in moving through
the shadow places that
a path to our most radiant,
reliable light is revealed.

If we were to come to each moment, to each other,
always not-wanting/not feeling wanted-from:

What magic could happen here
in this so very between place?

Opening to the biggest space
of what wants to come through us.

Opening to the deepest yearning—
the unformed energy,
the "only tending."

Choosing not to focus narrowly,
choosing not to seek something particular,
choosing not to go looking for anything.

Floating, drifting,
in not-wanting/not feeling wanted-from,

Still, available,
ready to be moved by Spirit and Soul.

Help create a safer, saner, more loving world:

Hug and speak softly to your self
  whenever you feel sad or hurt.

  Go more slowly
  and be more gentle with your self
    whenever you feel fearful or anxious.

  Listen carefully
  and take your self more seriously
    whenever you feel angry or resentful.

Be kind and generous with your self whenever
your best isn't as open-hearted or wonderful as
you wish it would be.

Celebrate and applaud your self whenever you
treat your self as lovingly as you'd treat anyone
else you truly care about.

41

Some thoughts on Mother's Day

Like so many of us who were raised by cold, uncaring, mean, neglectful or abusive mothers, every upcoming Mother's Day was a painful trial for me. Standing at the card rack, reading through endless Mother's Day cards searching for a card I could actually send to the woman who birthed me, I'd weep in anguish. I'd feel overwhelmed by grief and longing for what I'd never had, for what the cards suggested everyone else must have had: a loving, tender, caring and beloved mom.

For the first 30 years of my life, until my mother died, I continued to treat my self as uncaringly and critically as she had; I knew no better. Once she died, I was led to begin the journey to becoming a loving, compassionate, fiercely protective mother to the abandoned, love-starved child inside me.

Along the way of this remarkable journey, something magical unfolded. The Great Mother and Spirit Grandmothers came to enfold and support me and the fledgling Mommy-Inside that I was growing for my self.

So, on this special day, I celebrate and give thanks for their gifts to me.

Healing the wounds of mean mothering

1: The toxic legacy of mean mothering

Those of us who were raised by cold, critical, emotionally or physically abusive, unavailable and/or neglectful mothers almost inevitably find our selves tyrannized by vitriolic inner critics. These vicious, undermining voices lead those of us with such histories to treating our selves in the same damaging ways our mothers have treated us.

Despite how we try or what seeming wonders we accomplish in our lives, these undermining voices keep us from ever feeling we are truly worthy or lovable. Their litany can also keep us feeling shamed and diminished by any needs we might have that we cannot deal with on our own. We feel we are never enough or else that we are too much/overwhelming. We keep searching for what magical thing we might do that could finally silence those inner voices that denigrate everything we do. Nevertheless, each such thing, once achieved, becomes value-less; the critical onslaught continues unabated.

Similarly, no matter how many other people value and love us, no matter how many accolades we garner along the way, it does nothing to invalidate the belief in our essential unworthiness. As the saying goes: "Why would I want to join any club that would have me as a member?"—we believe that anyone that treasures our flawed selves is either stupid or deranged or not seeing clearly when they value us or tell us we are lovable. It's a terrible plight, this toxic legacy of wounding by damaged and damaging mothers that leaves us feeling so unworthy, so undeserving of love.

Those of us with this heritage are legion and, it seems, almost everywhere in the developed world. That so many women who mother are themselves so damaged, speaks volumes about the soul-destroying cultures in which almost all women are raised.

2: How the wounding happens

We come into this life totally dependent, with (I and others believe) an organismic trust that we will be welcomed and loved (with what these days is called healthy attachment). When we are met with less than that, our infant selves begin adapting to preserve what little might be available. (An example from my own life: my body remembers staying quiet, lying miserably cold and wet in my crib because the one who came when I cried would jerk me about roughly with sharp poking fingernails. When I waited quietly for her to come when she felt like it, I would not be treated as roughly.)

We begin, even before we have words or concepts for it, to believe that it is our failure, our lack that is the cause of our deprivation or mistreatment. We start on the road to trying to be better/gooder girls/more of whatever we think might unlock the loving we are not getting from our mothers.

By believing it is we who are lacking, we can keep holding onto the hope that, should we only find the key, the right way to be, our mothers will finally love us as we yearn to be loved. Were we to understand that the absence of that love has rather to do with the damage in them that leaves them unable to love us, we would lose all hope. To feel our helplessness, the futility of our desperate attempts to be lovable in the face of their lack of the capacity to love, is too devastating to tolerate. With a convoluted kind of loyalty, we as children, and later as adults, take-the-rap, finding presumed inadequacies in our selves to account for the unloving behavior from these damaged mothers: e.g., we are too needy, too ugly, too clumsy, too fat, too stupid. Our vicious inner critics keep the myth alive and keep us ever striving and always failing to feel worthy just as we are.

Often we go on to choose partners who treat us as our mothers treated us. This affirms the myth of our unworthiness, keeping us loyal to our mother's image: "See, no one can love me any better than she did, it must be me that's the problem."

3: Beginning the journey of healing the woundedness

It's sad but true that, if we didn't get the loving mothering, valuing and acceptance we all need and deserve as children, no amount of it coming from outside can reach through the time warp to our wounded inner little ones. Only when the who we are now has developed a relationship with those little ones and is already giving that love to our selves, can others' love come in to support our current self in that re-mothering process.

The work of healing from/transforming this terrible legacy begins with accepting that, at this stage of life, we must learn to provide for our selves the loving for which we yearn: it's an inside job. It requires letting go of the hope that what we craved and continue to crave can ever come from anywhere else. As we work at this difficult and painful letting go, we simultaneously begin turning inward to listen for and to the love-starved, abandoned and neglected little ones within us.

Letting go of the hope of ever getting it from the outside is one of the hardest things we ever have to do. As we let go, we may feel enormous grief at the finally acknowledged, irretrievable loss. We may feel furious for having been ripped off of our birthright and for having spent so many years fruitlessly contorting our selves, looking outward instead of inward for the love and acceptance we need to thrive. These are the feelings that we have held at bay by our continuing to hope.

Allowing, and providing safe space for these storms of emotion as they arise and pass through us, we begin the process of turning inward, of opening our ears and our hearts to the pain of the inner little ones that we, our selves, have continued neglecting all these years. In this practice of sitting-as-two, our grown-up, functioning adult self becomes available to hear and engage with the little ones' emotions and needs. This is the gateway to developing our capacity to lovingly re-mother these inner little ones, to developing an inner-good-mommy/caregiver.

4: A path to healing the mean mother woundedness

The journey of re-mothering our abandoned, neglected, wounded and shamed inner little ones can begin with us carving out some small regular bits of time (as little as five minutes twice a week can be a good start) and some safe, private space for inviting them to come and share their feelings with us. It can be helpful, in whatever way appeals to us, to make that space feel sacred, special for just these meetings.

It may take a while to hear from the little ones, they need to know that they can trust we really mean to be there for them if/when they show up. A good way to start each time is by apologizing to our little one(s) for having ignored them and their feelings for so long. Reassuring them that, even though we are feeling quite awkward and uneasy with all this, we are committed to developing a caring con-nection with them and hearing both how they feel and what they need from us. It can also be helpful to ask them to let us know what they need from us in order to feel safe enough to come out to visit and talk with us.

Sometimes, once they trust we really mean to hear them, they will simply speak in our hearts. Still, having fat colored pens and a blank drawing pad or journal available in which to write or draw (using our non-dominant hand) can provide a tangible way for the little ones to communicate with us using written words or images.

We may simply use journaling to dialog with these cut-off parts of our selves. We practice speaking to and treating our neglected inner selves with the loving they've never received. In this practice, we are developing a loving-inner-mommy/caregiver voice. Often, this loving voice is the one with which we speak to anyone we love and care about when they're suffering or upset. We already have the voice. What we need now is to find/give our selves the permission to use it with our very own selves.

We need to remember to remind our selves to be patient—it can be very slow going. And, we need to remember to remind our selves to applaud every baby step along the way of our developing relationship with these little inner selves.

5: The possibility of transforming the inner critic

We weather the storms of grief and rage over giving up the hope that we can ever get—from outside of our selves—the loving for which we've hopelessly yearned all our lives. Then, we dedicate our selves to developing and expanding our capacity to consistently and whole-heartedly make space for, connect with, listen to and tenderly practice re-mothering our (until now) disowned, love-starved little inner selves. We, at long last, are finding the unconditional love we've hungered for: we are giving it to our selves. We know in our bones that love is not something one ever needed to earn—it is grace, our birthright just for being alive, and our own loving inner-mother is, albeit belatedly, now bestowing it upon us.

Sometimes, along the way, we can even begin to engage with and embrace our inner critic with tenderness and caring. We understand that her mistreatment of us has been her way to keep us safe from abandonment: keeping us believing the myth that it is we who are/were unlovable/unworthy rather than that our damaged mothers were simply incapable of loving us.

As we embrace this misguided internalized mean mother/inner critic, we can help her gradually to let go of this terrible, now outdated, role that she's had. Treating her with gentleness, we comfort her when she rears her head out of fear that we are endangering our selves by breaking the code of loyalty to our mean mother's image of us, by seeing our selves as lovable and worthy. We remind her that we no longer have to protect our damaged, broken mothers by crippling our selves in order not to be abandoned. We remind her that we are safe now, that we will never abandon or stop loving our selves, even when we may not be at our most shining.

As we gradually become the fiercely protective, unconditionally loving mothers to our selves that we wish we'd had, we can maybe even grow into feeling compassion for the impaired, emotionally limited mothers we had. We can, perhaps, come to accept that they did the best they could with the consciousness available to them—even though it was far from what we needed.

And, maybe we cannot come to that place. Either way is okay.

Please note: Certainly, cold, critical, emotionally, physically or sexually abusive, unavailable and/or neglectful fathering leaves us with a legacy of both similar and different kinds of woundings and challenges to our feeling worthy and lovable. Blessed to have had a gentle, loving and compassionate father, I can't speak to these issues from a place of knowing-from-experience and that's the only place from which I can write authentically.

Listening to the voice of our inner knowing,
allowing our heart's wisdom always to guide us,
we come to recognize and commit
to following our own true path.

Living fully from this center of what is so for us,
we become evermore self-determining, resilient;
less and less susceptible to the tyrannies
of what convention or other people
might declare is the "right" way
for us to feel, to be or to act.

With gentle grace and compassion,
we move away from those
whose discomfort with our choices
leads them to challenge
or undermine our commitment
to living into the fullness
of exactly who and how we are
in this and every moment.

Cultivate the courage to embrace
whatever is unfolding in your life
and whatever cranky, hating feelings
you may feel about it.
Hold your precious self
with tender compassion as you do.

Being fully present with all of this
opens the way for change to happen,
for the next step to reveal itself.

Remember always:
every moment is sacred,
every task a teaching,
everything we embrace transforms.

Our beings move always
in the direction of growth.
Ever evolving,
the seeds of our next steps
germinate in our deeps —
even when the process
is invisible.

No need for vigilance
or pushing —
these only disrupt
the organic flow
of our unfolding.

Instead, we learn
to practice gentleness
and patient allowing,
remembering
to trust that
growth and change
are our true nature.

There are seasons when our
unfolding seems to be moving in
geologic time – at the pace with
which lichen transform boulders
back to crumbling soil.

In these seasons we become ever
more passionate in our devotion
to dancing our surrender into
just-this-moment.

With great compassion and
sympathy we gather to us and
lovingly embrace each of the
frustrated, angry, apprehensive,
disappointed, despairing, bereft
and overwhelmed selves who,
persistently clamoring, come with
us into just-this-moment.

We take time to welcome,
acknowledge, include and listen
heartfully to each upset self.
We wrap each in loving arms
and murmur to her words of
comfort and acceptance of
her just as and where she is.

Feeling deeply heard and
much beloved each – in her
own turn and finger by finger
– gradually unclenches her
hold on the expectations,
agendas, judgments, fears,
catastrophizings or griefs
she has brought with her into
just-this-moment.

The clamor slowly quiets. All of our
selves come together. We dance in
the paradox: embracing is releasing,
releasing is embracing, in
just-this-moment.

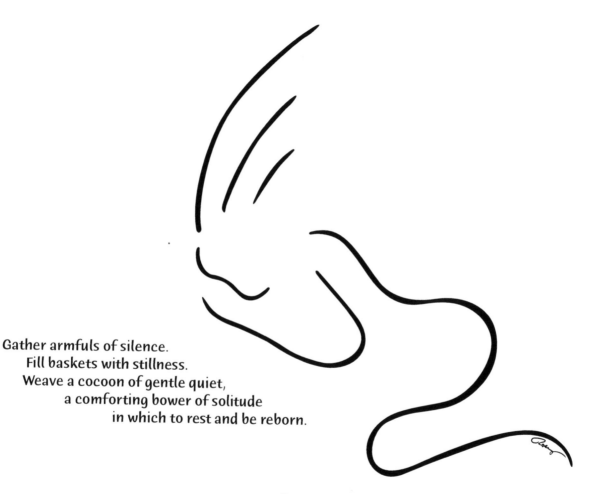

Gather armfuls of silence.
  Fill baskets with stillness.
    Weave a cocoon of gentle quiet,
      a comforting bower of solitude
        in which to rest and be reborn.

When Spirit/our Deep Self calls us
to open to new ways of being,
feelings of confusion and loss
are often stirred.

We allow the grief
as we honor,
give gratitude to
and gently begin
releasing the who we
have known our selves to be.

Tenderly, we invite
our selves to move
toward embracing
the who we are
becoming.

In birthing the fruit,
the flower
from which it is born
falls away.

Where the sun's light illuminates the edge
of darkness, rainbows are born.

Where the loving light of our own
compassion illuminates the darkness
within, healing, wholeness
and peace are born.

When the way forward
is not yet visible,
hold your precious self tenderly.
Embrace the not-knowing
with gentle compassion.

Calm the worrier-within
with soothing tales
of earlier fallow seasons
that led always to blossomings forth.

Dare not to clutter the empty time
with the noise of busyness for its own sake.
Whatever may be germinating deep within
needs open, quiet space in which to grow.

Dare not to push the process,
it will take as long as it needs to take.
Pushing disrupts the organic flow.
Practice patience; cultivate stillness.

Commit to radical trust.
Your Deep Self/Spirit
will lead you always
to the right-for-you next step
just exactly when you're ripe to move ahead.

In soft whisperings from the heart
the Child Within offers you always
the thread of your truth…

May you cherish that Child,
trust that voice
and weave that thread richly
into the fabric of your days.

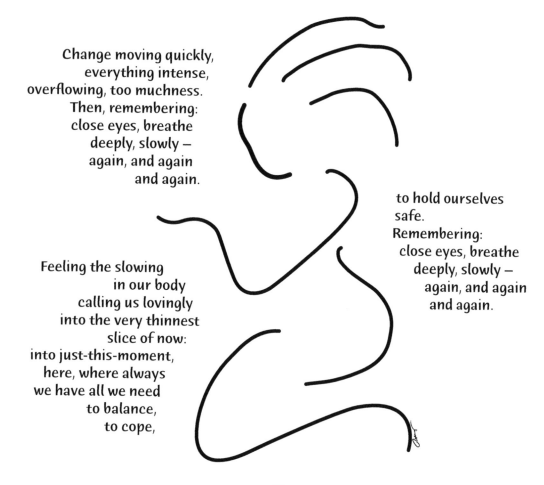

Change moving quickly,
everything intense,
overflowing, too muchness.
Then, remembering:
close eyes, breathe
deeply, slowly —
again, and again
and again.

Feeling the slowing
in our body
calling us lovingly
into the very thinnest
slice of now:
into just-this-moment,
here, where always
we have all we need
to balance,
to cope,

to hold ourselves
safe.
Remembering:
close eyes, breathe
deeply, slowly —
again, and again
and again.

73

Moving only as
fast as the slowest part
of her feels safe to go…

She honors and embraces
her vulnerabilty.

75

What is at the edge
is always the beginning
of new directions.

There is no "right" way…
only the way that we choose.

There is no "right" time…
only that which feels timely.

There are no "consequences"…
only the way things evolve.

Dancing at the edge
is a delicate dance
of balance…

of merging and emerging
in the "no-place"

between words and images,

between silence and sound,

between what is dying away
and what is coming to be.

In this birthing place
of the future,

remember to be gentle,
kind and tender with your self.

About what gets called selfish

When anyone says, "you're being selfish," we typically stop in our tracks, often feeling somewhat ashamed or suddenly not-okay about the behavior or choice that's being called selfish.

Like other words/ascriptions used by the dominant (white male system) culture to negatively reframe women's self-empowering behaviors, selfish is a word that Anne Wilson-Schaef (in her best selling book, *Women's Reality*) would classify as a "stopper." Stoppers are those words/reframes that, in knee-jerk fashion, quickly stifle behaviors in women that are perceived as threatening the status quo.

So, here's an antidoting, alternative reframing of the word:

When someone tells you that your behavior/choice is selfish, try immediately asking your self (or, if you feel up to it, the person) what it is that they want you to do instead of what you are doing. Or, alternately, why they want/need you to stop doing what you're doing.

Calling someone's behavior or choice selfish is actually a disguised way of manipulating someone's behavior to be more aligned with the wants/needs of the person who is calling the behavior selfish. It's really insidious shorthand for "You're not doing what I want you to do!" Consider remembering this when you hear someone (or your own inner critical voice) say that you're acting selfishly.

And, the deeper, overarching truth is that selfish is *not* a dirty word and being self-ish is *not* a negative way to be. When we are acting self-ish, we usually are acting to take the very best care of our selves; it's an act *for* our selves and *not against* anyone else. When we take the very best care of our selves, we don't need to manipulate others into taking care of us. And, when we need something we're unable to provide for our selves, we can ask—directly/openly—for what we need, fully willing to take the risk that the other person may say they can't or won't be able to provide whatever we've asked for.

Women have traditionally been expected to place everyone else's needs before our own. Except in the case of our (not-yet-adult) children, this expectation sorely needs to be re-examined and questioned. Remember, when we do what takes the best care of our selves, we have the energy and room to take into account and tend to others' needs in a much more healthy way.

Consider this reframing when next your own inner critical voice or anyone outside your self calls your behavior/choice "selfish!"

About mistakes

From the beginnings of her emergence, the Mommy-Inside me lovingly assured me that mistakes are things that happen in everyone's lives, frequently: "no one can do everything right all of the time," she said. She's helped me to understand a whole lot about so-called mistakes. They do not make us bad or wrong. They are nothing about which we have to feel shamed or humiliated. They can provide us with chances to learn more about what we're involved in or about what we're trying to do. They give us the opportunity to stretch and grow. If we're afraid of mistakes, we rob our selves of the adventure of exploring our furthest edges. Fixing a mistake sometimes opens us to whole new possibilities, to waking up our inventiveness and creativity. Sometimes, what looks like a mistake is really a doorway-in-disguise that leads to something unexpected and magical and nourishing.

When I make mistakes these days, even the really big ones involving clients or hurting someone's feelings, I still feel very sorry to have done that. I'm able to listen easily and caringly to everything the person has to say to me about the pain/upset my actions (words or inaction) have set in motion. I can listen openly even when they might be very furious with me. I'm able to take responsibility for and able to own the truth of what I did/said/didn't do. I'm able to express my deepest, most sincere regret for having created, by my words/actions/inaction, the space for such pain and grief. And, I'm willing and able to look—with the other person or just with my self—at what there is that I might do to make amends or how I might avoid making the same mistake again.

What I no longer do is feel like a terrible, worthless person. Nor do I feel shamed or humiliated. Nor do I feel that everything good about me is invalidated by this misstep. Nor do I berate and verbally abuse myself for simply being a fallible human being.

When we can acknowledge that we might well have done something terrible, without falling into feeling we're a terrible person, we're so much more available to the person we've injured. We can make room to fully hear their upset and anger. We can be listening attentively instead of trying to defend, justify or explain our selves as they are trying to express themselves to us. And, we don't contribute the tangle of creating a situation in which the one we have injured feels that sharing their upset will be devastating to our self-esteem. This allows a healing to happen. Be especially gentle and loving with your fallible, mistake-making simply human self.

In the between-times,
when we're no longer
who we've been
and not yet
who we are becoming,
we practice letting go
of expectations,
timetables,
judgments.

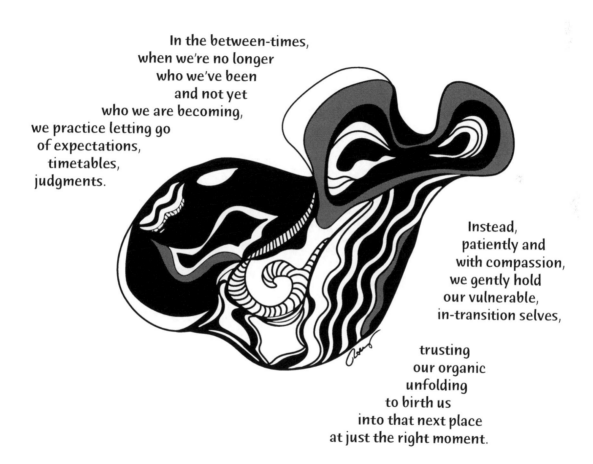

Instead,
patiently and
with compassion,
we gently hold
our vulnerable,
in-transition selves,

trusting
our organic
unfolding
to birth us
into that next place
at just the right moment.

In the sacred act of resting…She nourishes her deepest self.

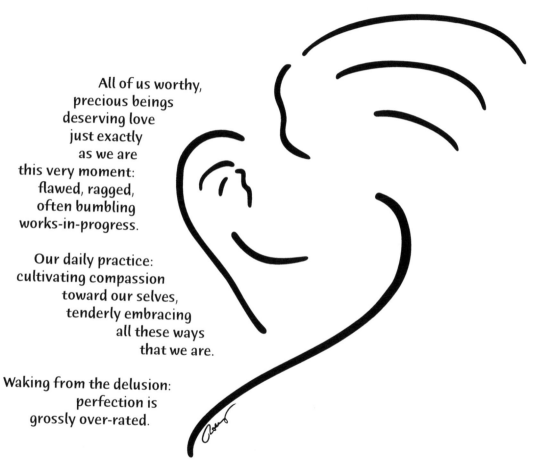

All of us worthy,
precious beings
deserving love
just exactly
as we are
this very moment:
flawed, ragged,
often bumbling
works-in-progress.

Our daily practice:
cultivating compassion
toward our selves,
tenderly embracing
all these ways
that we are.

Waking from the delusion:
perfection is
grossly over-rated.

Opening to the wisdom
of her body and
her "belly" feelings...

She celebrates
her deepest inner-knowing place.

Cherishing all the
parts of her self with
tender, gentle kindness…

She feeds that which
hungers within her.

It does not matter whether how we are in the moment
is born from our woundings or our
wholeness.

What matters is how lovingly,
compassionately and
unconditionally we
can embrace how
we are in the moment;
how patiently dedicated
we can be to providing
safety for our slowest,
most fearful parts.

With this embracing and
dedication, we create the
fertile inner soil that nourishes
our continued blossoming and unfolding.

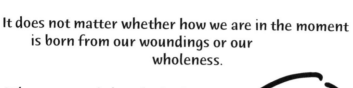

Be kind and gentle with all the parts of your self.

Move only as quickly as the slowest part of you feels safe to go.

Listen for and embrace the deep inner truths speaking through your fearful, angry and mean-spirited feelings.

Practice sharing your truths openly, everywhere, as if you believe that being authentic is what really matters.

Remember that loving your self unconditionally is a revolutionary act and that acknowledging your vulnerability is an act of power.

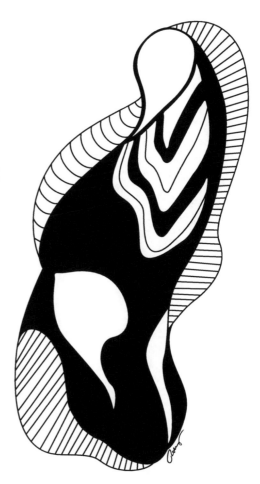

Is it really procrastination or is it something else entirely?

When we don't seem to be able to get to doing something we or others think we should be doing in what we or they think is a timely manner, we and/or they call it procrastinating. A behavior we all unquestioningly view as worthy of criticism; a fault in need of being corrected. But, what happens if we look at this not-being-able-to-do some particular thing as an important message from our deep self?

Many of us already get and accept that angry, nasty or mean-spirited thoughts/feelings arise in us when something not-good-for-us is going on. When these feelings flood us, we've learned to consider them as signals/messages from within our deeps asking us to look for what it is in what's happening that we need to address, communicate about or remove our selves from.

What we call procrastinating can be looked at in the very same light. Namely, when we can't seem to get our selves in gear to do some particular thing, instead of criticizing our selves (or accepting anyone else's criticism) about this behavior, we look for what message our Deep (authentic) Self might be trying to give us.

Experience teaches me, over and over again, that when I'm not getting to something I (or others) think I should be doing, it's either the wrong time for me to be doing it or, sometimes, the wrong thing for me to be doing at all. When I embrace my not-doing behavior compassionately—with curiosity and inquiry instead of criticism—I always learn something important about my own needs. With this information, I can take better care of me and be more mindful in making commitments to others

See what you think and consider trying this re-framing the next time you're giving your self a bad time about not yet getting to something you (or someone else or the world-in-general) think you should already have been doing.

It's important to remember that what our culture calls the socialization process is quite often a curriculum that teaches us to ignore our inner knowings in order to behave in so-called socially acceptable ways. This ignoring always damages us, moving us off our center. Our work is to honor these inner truths and find ways to walk them creatively and safely out in the world.

In the feeling stuck times, remember the magic of being human

Our being, by its very nature, moves always in the direction of growth, evolving moment by moment even when the process is feeling invisible and the steps are microscopic.

Growth and forward motion continue whether we are vigilant or not.

Pushing our selves often slows the process: it stirs resistance in the healthy parts of us that are protecting the natural flow from being overthrown or interfered with.

When things feel really hard, slowing way down allows the internal, organic balancing process to work its magic.

When you get scared that you'll never come out of this (or any other place in which you find your self) remember that everything in us moves always toward growth and change—no matter how it looks to our outside eye.

Some reflections on the challenges and teachings of aging

I was raised by a damaged, neglectful and emotionally abusive mother. My mother (as others of her ilk) responded to any of my needs for help or comfort with derision and shaming. I learned early on that there was no one outside my self to safely rely on: I had either to provide me with anything I might need or simply do without whatever it might be. In order to survive, I became fiercely independent, convinced it was demeaning to need any sort of help or support from the outside world. I was equally convinced that such needs would never be met, anyway.

Those of us with such backgrounds—or any other of the myriad background experiences in our society that lead women to become fiercely independent and self-empowered—found that our natures served us well through many years of our lives. We often became successful and effective in the business and profes-sional worlds despite, or perhaps because of, their ingrained sexism. We were seen as strong, dependable (like men) rather than vulnerable (like women) in a culture where vulnerability has long been seen as weakness and inferior.

For our cohort, aging brings a special set of challenges. I'd long understood that there would come a time when doing-it-my-self or doing-without would cease to be a viable life strategy. I'd decided that I would deal with the need to shift from my life-long comfort zone only if or when circumstances forced me to do something different and not a moment before then.

The time for shifting came when, at 71, I broke my first bone—my right elbow (surgical repair necessary)—in a fall just blocks from my home. Oddly enough, for the previous two months—in the interests of fostering brain plasticity—I had been doing as many things as I could with my left hand. Alas, despite how adept I'd become at using that hand for most of the so-called activities-of-daily-life, there were lots of other chores beyond my one-handed capabilities. So began several weeks of being forced into finding my way to be comfortable with asking for and receiving help. It was quite a stretch.

I moved between frustration, crabbiness and tears as I tried creating solutions to enable me to still manage my life on my own, one-handed. Over and over again, I had to surrender and (as it felt to me then) submit to asking for help. Needing help meant having to explain how I wanted (thought I needed) things done. Given that I'm very particular (a bit OCD) about how I do almost everything, this felt like a lot of work. It also seemed like something that could strain the patience of the people I might ask for help. And, it all felt embarrassing.

Fortunately, for my beleaguered psyche, I had the funds to be able to hire a woman I'd known for years who was then doing eldercare. And, even more fortunately, she's someone as particular about everything as I am, and a quick study to boot. Paying her for her time allowed me to feel safer about asking for and receiving help. Friends still pitched in for many things, but Valerie handled the basics most days. Even with her by my side, I'd still automatically start to try to do things myself. She'd put a hand on my arm and gently say, "Robyn, that's what you're paying me for, let me do it." Then, we'd laugh together.

Gradually, asking friends for help around the edges became less fraught. Knowing they knew I had Valerie as my mainstay, I could trust that they wouldn't overextend and then be resentful for feeling they had to help whether they felt like it or not. It was an ongoing struggle against the undertow of the early damage from being humiliated about having needs. One dear friend brought me to tears when she said, "You don't realize it, dear heart, but it's truly a gift you're giving me when you ask for, allow and receive my help!"

When, a year later, I tripped (again just blocks from home) and caused a hairline fracture of the knob of my hip (no surgery necessary), I saw how much easier/less embarrassing it had become for me to ask for the help I needed. Still, being able again to hire Valerie for the basics eased the way.

The two falls-that-caused-fractures in two years confronted me with another set of the-challenges-of-living-in-an-aging-body. For over 25 years, I had spent many of my days wandering alone along the front-country trails in Ojai. I carried a friend's expired cell phone believing that I could use it to call 911 if I got into trouble while alone in the wild places. When I'd finally, a few years back, bought a flip phone, I'd discovered that there was no reception on any of my favorite trails. That earlier discovery combined with these two falls (even though they both had happened in town) seemed to be a wake-up call. I understood that it was no longer safe to go off on those solitary hikes that had so nourished my soul. While I could always trust the Grandmothers to protect me, it was up to me to reduce my exposure to risk.

I felt frustrated and furious, sad and bereft. It was hard to imagine life without the freedom to wander alone on the trails. Hiking with a friend, even if we did that in silence, didn't feel like an alternative. What I'd yearned for (and been fed by) was complete solitude in those wild places—the feeling of being the only human on the planet. I grieved the loss deeply, had many tantrums and lots of tears. At the same time, I understood that I would have to find my way to accepting and embracing this *new normal*. Just as I'd had to embrace the *new normal* of having to be okay with needing to ask for and receive help. In time, I actually discovered that wandering along the tide-lines at our wild beaches or along our tree-lined town streets late at night could both give me some of the feeling I was missing.

Living in temporarily-able, aging bodies—despite all we may choose to be doing to hold back the aging process—asks us to be willing to be more tender and gentle with our selves. Our landscape keeps changing; we're faced with the challenges of a succession of *new normals* that we need to come to accept and embrace. On the way to that acceptance, though, it's essential that we allow our selves the space to be with whatever rage and grief comes up: to rail, rant, be sad and cry as long and as often as those feelings arise. Only intermittently during, or (more likely) on the far side of the emotional storms, can we begin to embrace the changes.

In a culture as emotion-phobic and ageist as ours, allowing our feelings to fulminate and honoring the changes in our precious aging bodies can be daunting! We need each other's support on this journey.

Please note: Surely, aging men also have to cope with the challenges of losing lifelong independence as well as with their own ever-changing *new normals*. But, as with my writings about the legacy of mean mothering, I can't speak to these issues from a place of knowing-from-experience and that's the only place from which I can write authentically.

Questioning the push to always maintain an attitude-of-gratitude

Just as I'm troubled by the ambient hype around forgiveness, so-called selfishness and so-called procrastination, I'm intensely reactive to the whole cultural and New Age flap around gratitude. All too often—despite various research evidence that indicates cultivating an-attitude-of-gratitude has a positive effect emotionally—the push for us to list what we're grateful for when we're actually feeling in pain or put upon is simply one more instance of our emotion-phobic culture's pressure to get us to stop our selves from feeling our upset/distress/anger. Years of working, both with healing my self and with others on their own healing journeys, make it clear to me that challenging feelings need to be felt-through, not shut off by immediately shifting to so-called positive thinking/attitude.

Rather than buying into the hype around gratitude, I find it much more healing to invite my hurting, angry, grieving, distressed self to immerse those parts of me in these feelings until I'm done with them for the moment. Only then do I look around for the magic, the teachings, the wisdom that may be harvested from my having been through the particular challenging experience: I open to seeing/feeling/being grateful for the magic that seems like Spirit/the Grandmothers having a hand in whatever—good or hard—is unfolding in my life.

Being open to recognizing, acknowledging and giving thanks for the gifts/magic in our lives is certainly important to our sense of well-being. Yet, so is our availability to making space to feel/plumb the depths of our pain, grief, disappointment and anger whenever these feelings arise in us.

Is forgiving really essential to moving forward/growing? Does it really get to the heart of the matter?

Allowing our selves to feel our anger, pain, sense of betrayal, upset or outrage is actually what's essential to our healing and growth. Making safe space to fully experience and vent all of the energy of those feelings—by our selves, *not* on someone and without judging our selves for feeling/doing so—is what heals us. Carving such space out of our busy lives can be enormously challenging, so we may have to do this process in small, intermittent bits and snatches. This will still work.

It takes as long as it takes, though much less time *if we fully embrace rather than judge our right to have these feelings.*

New Age (as well as Christian) precepts warn us that it's only by forgiving those who've wronged us that we can move on and grow our selves or be good people. In response, we pressure our selves to let go of our anger and upset at those who've hurt us, we force our selves to be okay with whatever it is/was. When we do

111

this, the truth (as I see it) is that we are actually further violating/wounding our already violated/wounded selves.

Furthermore, currently popular New Age "law of attraction" flap would have us believe that "feeling such [so-called negative] feelings will only draw more of the same to us." *But, shutting off these feelings when they arise forces them below the level of our awareness where their energy continues to affect our bodies or beings.*

Those who've physically, sexually and/or emotionally abused us, in childhood or as adults, have treated our precious selves in truly unacceptable and unforgivable ways. As we allow our selves to feel and know this, we can—at the same time—come to a place of recognizing that *these misguided perpetrators were doing the best they could with the consciousness available to them. We can see them as emotionally crippled beings. We can understand that they were unable to act differently.* Still, we do not need to pardon, excuse, absolve or exonerate their acts *even* as we understand that what they did was all they were capable of doing at the time.

Compassionately acknowledging, honoring and taking the most gentle care of our precious and wounded self/spirit is what helps us to heal.

Slip the traces of containment.
Loose the fetters of constraint.
Dissolve the boxes that constrict.

Celebrate your radiance.
Consecrate your confusion.
Embrace your disowned shadow places.

Practice living fully in the middle
of your beautiful, magical, still evolving,
sometimes lost, not always shining
all-of-who-you-are-right-now self…

Feeling vibrantly full-of-our-selves
– miraculous, imperfect works-in-progress
that we are – is everyone's birthright!

113

Delighting in all the
baby steps along the way
of her journey…

She celebrates the
wonder of her
unfolding.

115

From the core,
energy rising,
vibrating,
burgeoning forth,
stretching us,
cracking us open,
unfurling wings
we did not know we'd had.
Lifted on gusts of joy,
we are soaring
beyond the furthest reaches
of any self we have known.

Bask in her sunshine,
  dance with her moon,
  revel in her mountains,
  December and June.
  Flow with her rivers,
  ocean tides out and in.
  Delight in her spiders,
  watching as they spin.
  Openhearted wander
in her sacred breast.
Receive from the Mother
  her loving so blessed.
  Deep in our hearts,
  her compassionate voice
  recalls to us always
  that we have a choice:
  to slow down, to soften
  to open the space
  to welcome the Mother —
  magic, rapture and grace.

Everyday magic: noticing the moments when Spirit has clearly had a hand in it

While meandering home from dinner in town (a matter of seven modest-length blocks) at about 9:00 PM one night not too long ago, I suddenly realized I hadn't a clue where I was. Nothing seemed familiar. I thought I was on one street but the street sign seemed to say I was somewhere else. Then, I realized I couldn't even make sense of the street sign posts, baffled by whether the street I was on was the one inscribed on the upright post or the one inscribed on the cross arm. I felt thoroughly disoriented and confused.

A worried little voice in my head whispered, "Oh my, getting lost in familiar surroundings is one of the first signs of Alzheimer's!" My Mommy-Inside's response was immediate: "Honey, we don't need to think about that right now, we just have to find our way home and I promise we will." So—fairly calmly—I kept meandering, on the lookout for any familiar landmarks, fairly certain that I'd eventually find my way.

After a bit, I did, indeed, figure out where I was and how to get home. What would normally have been a ten to twelve minute stroll stretched to almost forty minutes by the time I got to my corner. As I approached the intersection at the entry to my little one-block-long cul-de-sac, there were four County Sheriff's Department SUVs parked at the corners of the cross street and three Ojai Police cars parked in my block. Several uniformed officers were milling about the block. Some around two young men outside a pick-up truck across the street from my house and a couple of others talking with the occupants of a car parked flush up against my front fence gate.

As I walked into my block, I stopped an officer who was leaving to ask what was happening, saying I had gotten a bit turned around on my way home. He said it was all over. Though, had I gotten there earlier, he said, I'd have walked into the middle of a very intense domestic altercation. It wasn't one of my neighbors, he told me. Rather, it was something between two groups of young people who'd come up from Ventura and randomly landed on my street.

(The next day, I learned from a neighbor that she had been awakened at around 9:00 the night before by very frightening, angry yelling. Clearly that fighting had been taking place right in front of my house.)

As I walked around to my unblocked side gate, I overheard another officer telling the people in the car blocking my front gate that the he appreciated both their and the other participants respectful responses to the police. He told them that all too often, with domestic altercations, the combatants turn their aggression on the police responders.

Once inside my house, I doubled over laughing. "Those Grandmothers!" I thought, "They take such good care of me, if sometimes in the oddest ways!" I thanked them so much for keeping me from coming into the middle of the mess that had been. As I continued laughing, I thought, "There's sooo much magic in my life!" And, then, I thought, "There's likely just as much magic in everyone's lives—the thing is whether we notice it as it unfolds."

These days, when I almost trip and then don't fall, I thank the Grandmothers. When I snuggle into my sleeping bag in my tent for the night, and something nudges me to go back into the house, where I discover I hadn't quite closed the refrigerator door before I left, I thank the Grandmothers. When I happen to look up beyond my computer screen to see two hummingbirds sharing (rather than fighting for) one feeding station by alternating: one drinking while the other has its head up swallowing and then reversing, I thank the Grandmothers for calling my attention to this amazing spectacle. When, while floating in my hot tub at night, I open my eyes and see a meteor streaking across the sky, I thank the Grandmothers for nudging me to open my eyes at just that second. In all these little magical moments, I feel their hand in it and I'm filled with awe and gratitude.

In a world that has become a place where there's so much that feels (and definitely is) wrong, where everything is always moving too fast, or getting in the way of our moving as fast as we've come to feel we need to move, it's hard to remember to remind our selves to slow down, to make room to notice the tiny bits of magic that are always around us. Yet, it's noticing these bits of magic that can be balm for our battered souls, especially in these crazy-making times.

Honoring our introversion in a culture that idealizes extroversion

Like so many of us, I revel in the quiet richness of solitude. I feel deeply nourished and replenished by the time I spend with only my self as company. Honoring my voracious hunger for this kind of time, I've designed a life that provides me with lots of it, regularly. Arranging this life has required owning, advocating for and celebrating my introversion in a culture that generally idealizes extroversion and—for the most part—pathologizes introversion.

(I think the most meaningful definition of the difference between introversion and extroversion is that people on the introvert side of the continuum are replenished by solitude while those at the extrovert end are nourished more by social interactions. Truth be told, we all have some of each side of this continuum in us even as we define our selves more to one end than the other.)

Like many folks at the introvert side of the continuum, I'd rather have a root canal without anesthesia than attend a large social gathering or a dinner with more than a half dozen people. I've often felt like an alien in this world that values ways of being that make little sense to my spirit. In years past (before I became more selective of with whom I'd spend time when I felt like connecting), people in my life sometimes wondered if I might be depressed because I spent so much time alone. In those earlier days, I'd sometimes actually worry that there might be something wrong with me because I had such a strong preference for time alone and so little interest in the more socially acceptable time spent with others.

While I no longer worry about any of this, I still feel as though I live in a world whose values baffle and disturb me. Lately, I've been feeling crazed by the endless repetition of references to research which demonstrates how necessary strong social networks are for healthy aging. "How many self-described introverts were part of these studies?" I want to ask. Clearly, if one is an extrovert, social networks are crucial to wellbeing—otherwise one is apt to feel empty, lonely, bored and/or isolated. Yet, introverts—those of us who have rich inner lives—are rarely likely to feel empty or lonely or bored with our own solo company.

It really is possible to live into celebrating the healthy joys of introversion, solitude and the more contemplative lifestyle. Those of us who live and enjoy life at this end of the continuum (from 30 to 50% of the population depending on which statistic you credit) can choose to honor, more openly affirm and claim the juicy richness of this different path that we walk. It's a path that's existed for centuries and, until more recent years, been a valued thread in the tapestry of all life. The current cultural overvaluing/idealization of extroversion actually undermines the capacity for self-awareness and emotional fluency that allows one's soul to develop and flourish.

Happily there's been a recent spate of books to gather if one needs/wants support for this lifestyle. I particularly love this quote from one of these books: "You're not shy; rather, you appreciate the joys of quiet. You're not antisocial; instead, you enjoy recharging through time alone. You're not unfriendly, but you do find more meaning in one-on-one connections than large gatherings." —Laurie Helgoe

I particularly love the various titles of these books (which seem to be garnering a large readership—introverts of the world, unite!):

Susan Cain's *Quiet: The Power of Introversion in a World That Can't Stop Talking.*

Sophia Dembling's *Introvert's Way: Living a Quiet Life in a Noisy World.*

Laurie Helgoe's *Introvert Power: Why Your Inner Life is Your Hidden Strength.*

Nancy Okerlund's *Introverts at Ease: An Insider's Guide to a Great Life on Your Own Terms.*

Marti Olsen Laney's *The Introvert Advantage: Making the Most of Your Inner Strengths.*

Cheryl Card's *Discover the Power of Introversion: What Introverts are Never Told and Extraverts Learn the Hard Way.*

Over the years, I've learned that I am a gregarious hermit: an introvert who enjoys intimate sharing from time to time. With this, as with everything else about me that is somewhat different-from-the-acceptable-norm, I discover that when I'm true to my own nature—living from my own center/reality—what other people think or say about me clearly becomes their issue rather than mine. I've always loved Terry Cole Whittaker's famous line (and the title of her book) "What you think of me is none of my business!"

Tenderly, with so
much love, I practice
embracing my self in every
single moment of my living…

I practice being really gentle with my self, in as many ways and as often as I possibly can. Because no matter how it appears, I am a delicate, vulnerable creature who needs and deserves to be treated with gentleness.

I practice talking kindly, tenderly and lovingly to my self as much of the time as I possibly can. Because only this sort of talking will encourage me to take the steps I need to grow and thrive.

I practice finding ways and places in which to make it safe to feel all my feelings, even though the world dismisses their value.

I practice reminding my self that rest is a sacred act: as meaningful, significant, productive and necessary as any other purposeful act. Because remembering this will help me to choose rest in a world that devalues fallow time or space.

I practice finding and telling my self only those stories that allow me to feel that it's absolutely okay for me to be just as I am right now: a work-in-progress still continuing to grow, change and evolve.

Because knowing this truth — that I can
always feel okay about anywhere I am —
is what gives me the courage and strength
to take the risks that grow me.

I practice going only as fast as the slowest part
of me feels safe to go. Because this is the
only pace that is safe for me.

I practice listening to my body and my belly feelings.
Because they always let me know what is so for me.

Re-Membering Rest: A Sacred Celebration

To Rest…
> To take time out of time, to stop all talk and doing, to be still, empty

Is a Sacred Act…
> As essential as breathing; as significant, meaningful, honorable, productive as any other purposeful action; as critical, in this moment, as any of the other "more important" pulls that make it seem "there's no time to rest"

Of Profound Nourishment and Solace…
> A gift one gives one's soul, spirit, psyche, body, mind and heart; a necessary break in the momentum of living life from our more voluble conscious needs; a quiet space in which to be available to the softer voice of our Deep Self, our heart and belly wisdom

That Requires Courage and Trust…
> In the midst of a culture that over-whelmingly values more, bigger, further, faster, now; in the midst of an alternative culture that vibrates with the anguished urgency of ending all the poisonous ways, habits, and isms that mortally endanger our planet and all its beings; in the midst of a personal history that usually gives priority to creative acts with more immediate, tangible outcomes

Gentle, Dear Being, Rest Yourself, Now

Allowing the love of the
Great Mother to enfold her...

She remembers to more
lovingly mother and cherish
her self.

True selflessness and compassion flow
not so much from transcending
as from abundantly loving the self…

May you give your self (and the rest
of the beings on the planet) the gift of
loving your self more dearly and
generously in the days ahead.

About the author

I spent my first 32 years as a hyper-self-critical super-achiever never at peace with my self. Just past my 32nd birthday, at the urging of a voice deep within me, I dropped out of that life. I took to the road in a van I'd set up as a self-contained bed-sitting room/womb-space and began the journey of uncovering who I might be without the overlay of all my driven excelling.

Now in my late 70s, I'm delightedly living life in the slow lane, at peace (at last) with all the ways I am and am not. With two affectionate, quirky eleven-year-old kitties, I live in my recently purchased forever-home: a remodeled 1938 cottage in a cul-de-sac at the edge of the village of Ojai, with views of the surrounding mountains. In containers in my redwood-fenced front, side and back yards, I grow succulents, roses and edible greens. I feed goldfinch, hummingbirds and myriad seed-feeding birds, as well as the orioles that come only in spring and summer. I spend endless hours reading (in front of my fireplace, in the garden or in my hammock), floating in my hot tub or tending-the-temple, as I call my puttering around the house and garden. I walk around town (at night for peace or during the day for errands), along the tide lines of nearby beaches or—less frequently these days—on our local front country trails/fire roads. I sleep year round, but for rainy or windy days, in a windowed tent in my private backyard. I still see clients and mentor younger therapists for a few hours on two days every other week.

Writing and making art weave randomly through my days. My first book (*Go Only as Fast as Your Slowest Part Feels Safe to Go: Kindling Gentleness and Compassion for Our Exhausted Selves*) was birthed in a seven-year process of going only as fast as my own slowest part felt safe to go. A companion journaling workbook (*Tenderly Embracing All the Ways that I Feel and Am*) emerged—in collaboration with my close friend and tech mentor, Barbara Fosbrink—later that same year. For the past five years I've been on somewhat of a writing hiatus, no longer writing regular columns for my websites and only infrequently being nudged to write the occasional short essay. These essays are collected in this current book (*Choosing Gentleness: Opening Our Hearts to All the Ways we Feel and Are in Every Moment*) that was assembled in collaboration with Barbara and our graphic design wizard, Catherine Baker.

Robyn's availability

A California Licensed Psychologist, I have been working with clients since 1964. I'm available for open-ended, one-time or ongoing individual consultations by phone or in person in Ojai, California.

My commitment is to creating safe space in which to help people (re)connect with and honor the wisdom of their own inner knowing: the wisdom that can guide us to living life more in harmony with who we truly are, even in this crazy-making, invalidating world.

I work interactively, dedicated, as far as I'm able, to working in your personal idiom rather than pushing you to work in mine. My approach is eclectic, influenced by a strong feminist consciousness: I think it's important to note when and where noxious cultural influences are contributing to what ails us. A deep spiritual consciousness (not about God/Goddess or any particular religion or ism) is another element that I bring to the work: I believe we come into a body to do soul work and that we can experience our selves as more than merely victims if/when we see the challenges we're facing as opportunities to grow our selves/our souls.

Part of helping you (re)connect with your inner knowing involves having you be in charge both of how long we meet in any session and how often you choose to return. Each time we meet, we work until you reach some closure around the issue(s) you've brought to the session. Usually this comes when you have some clear ideas of what you might focus on as you continue the work on your own. The option of such organic closure allows your work to progress more efficiently. Some people use as little as 35 minutes a time while others use as much as three or four hours. At the end of each session, you pay/send a check for the time you've used, pro-rated at my current hourly fee.

If you'd like to talk about the possibility of arranging an individual consultation and check on my current fee, you can call me at 805-646-4518. Leave a message for me to call you back at a time that works for you (best make sure to give me a clue about in which time zone you live). Or, if you prefer, you can drop me an email at Robyn@compassionateink.com.

Appendix

Ordering information

Compassionate Ink is the publishing imprint through which Robyn offers her nourishing collection of resources celebrating going slowly, compassionately embracing all of our feelings, nurturing the Little Ones Inside and honoring the Sacred Feminine.

The forthelittleonesinside.com and the compassionateink.com websites host the words, images and tales Robyn has been creating over the years. These have all emerged from her dedicated life-long journey of healing (and helping others heal) from the harshness that our crazy-making world visits upon all of us, especially women. (Robyn L. Posin, Ph.D. is a licensed psychologist in private practice in Ojai, California.)

Go Only as Fast as Your Slowest Part Feels Safe to Go: Tales to Kindle Gentleness and Compassion for Our Exhausted Selves is also available in Kindle, iBook and Nook formats. After a first read of these emotionally uncensored, autobiographical healing tales, many open the book randomly in moments of unease, confusion or doubt and read the chapter to which they've opened as a message from Spirit/their Deep Self.

Tenderly Embracing All the Ways that I Feel and Am: Journaling to Kindle Gentleness and Compassion for Our Precious Selves is a natural extension of and companion to *Go Only as Fast as Your Slowest Part Feels Safe to Go.* A bound 8.5" x 11" journal, its otherwise blank pages are edged with words and images to inspire and invite you to kindle gentleness and compassion for your precious self as you write, draw, explore and reflect on your journey.

Choosing Gentleness: Opening Our Hearts to All the Ways We Feel and Are In Every Moment, is a collection of short essays and poems-with-drawings that encourage us to give our selves permission to be exactly how we are in every moment—to honor and embrace wherever we are in our process without criticism and to treat all of our feelings with tenderness and compassion.

Catalog of Treasures

Ordering information for the Remembering and Celebrations Cards, the deck of 64 bookmark-size cards that you've seen, paired with their tales, in *Go Only as Fast as Your Slowest Part Feels Safe to Go: Tales to Kindle Gentleness and Compassion for Our Exhausted Selves* can be found at www.compassionateink.com/catalog-of-treasuresalt. There you'll also find ordering information for Robyn's collection of healing note cards, postcards, poster cards and amulets.

50373342R10093

Made in the USA
Middletown, DE
25 June 2019